A Glimpse into Heaven

Relieve the pain of the loss of a loved one by understanding Heaven's beautiful truths…

by

Jennifer Holdstock

A Glimpse into Heaven

Copyright © 2019 by **Jennifer Holdstock**

All rights reserved. No part of this publication may be reproduced, distributed or transmitted in any form or by any means, without prior written permission.

Unless otherwise indicated, all scripture quotations are taken from the Amplified Bible (AMP) copyright © 1954,1958,1962,1964,1965,1987 by the Lockman Foundation. Used by permission. (www.lockman.org)

All illustrations by Madeleine W Pires (mfaithart.com)

A Glimpse into Heaven – Jennifer Holdstock- 1st ed.

Foreword

It has been a life-enhancing experience to help Jenny with this tender account of witnessing her mum "settling in" to heaven. This is revelation knowledge, supported by Bible verses. It is my belief that any reader, already familiar with the Word of God and the Holy Spirit, will know beyond a doubt that heaven is a real place – more real perhaps than this earth in the sense that it is eternal – and like I did, have so many things wondered about expanded upon, confirmed and affirmed. The waters of refreshing, the welcoming loved ones, the eyes of Jesus, the descriptions of the children and shining blades of grass were particularly encouraging for me. There is something wonderfully reassuring and strengthening for everyone in this book as Jenny shares the insights so graciously given to her by God.

Madeleine W. Pires
Editing Consultant and Illustrator
8th September 2020

"May Christ through your faith actually dwell (settle down, abide, make His permanent home) in your hearts! May you be rooted deep in love and founded securely on love,

That you may have the power and be strong to apprehend and grasp with all the saints [God's devoted people, the experience of that love] what is the breadth and length and height and depth [of it];

[That you may really come] to know [practically, through experience for yourselves] the love of Christ, which far surpasses mere knowledge [without experience]; that you may be filled [through all your being] unto all the fullness of God [may have the richest measure of the divine Presence, and become a body wholly filled and flooded with God Himself]!

Now to Him Who, by (in consequence of) the [action of His] power that is at work within us, is able to [carry out His purpose and] do superabundantly, far over and above all that we [dare] ask or think [infinitely beyond our highest prayers, desires, thoughts, hopes or dreams]-

To Him be glory in the church and in Christ Jesus throughout all generations forever and ever.

Amen"

Ephesians 3 17 - 21

CONTENTS

Introduction 7
About Mum 11
The Entwining of Two Realms 13
Love Transcends All Boundaries 23
Love Overcomes All 27
All of Heaven Anticipates 33
Arrived Home Safely! 37
Adventures in Heaven 43
Heavenly Home 49
Children were not Created to Suffer 55
Infants in Heaven 65
Encounter with Jesus 71
A Glimpse of the Workings of Praise 79
Salvation Prayer 89
About the Author 91

Introduction

I want to write this illustrative book which gives a detailed account of the revelations I received during the time of my mum's passing.

In most people's eyes, it is considered a sad loss when a family member dies. There is usually evident grief when a parent, who is dearly loved, moves from the earthly realm to the heavenly realm. It is presumed to be a time when grief is at the forefront of every waking moment, when thoughts of "how can I live without them prevail", instead of an understanding of the miraculous resurrection power that comes into play when a dear loved one transcends from Earth to Heaven. This is not just an idea of my own invention, but this is the same power that is described by the apostle Paul in Ephesians 1:19-20, which demonstrates God's almighty power applied in the resurrection of Christ,

> *"We can know and understand the immeasurable and the unlimited and surpassing greatness of His power... as demonstrated in the working of His*

> *mighty strength, which He exerted in Christ when He raised Him from the dead and seated Him at His own right hand in the heavenly places."*

The Bible says that this great power is accessible and is not something to be afraid of but is available to each and every one of us as we choose to believe.

I can genuinely say that being with my mother as she "died" and the subsequent revelations in the spirit have been the most amazing, phenomenal and beautiful experience that I think I will ever experience on this Earth. Yet you might be saying, "But how can you say that?"

Throughout this book, I will illustrate and put into words as directed by Holy Spirit - a small portion of this miraculous transitioning power and revelation of the world to come. However, the reader must consider that it is difficult at times, to express in language the visions of a world that is actually beyond human understanding. Therefore, I write this through human limitations albeit with a spirit that is bursting to show forth the beautiful, magnificent and glorious world to come through the visions that I have been privileged to experience.

As you read this book, I truly hope and pray that you will find it fascinating, intriguing and beautifully overwhelming. I pray also, that if you have lost dear friends and family members, that you will find this a source of comfort and perhaps even a change of perspective. I want to reassure you that you will indeed be able to see them fully engaged in the activities of Heaven, ever loved, ever safe and ever surrounded... by Him who created all life.

Introduction

Thank you for taking the time to read this book. I pray you will be inspired, changed and empowered to do great exploits for Him, as our friend, Holy Spirit reveals the realms of Heaven in new and amazing ways. I take no credit for any of the words written in this book: I give all the credit to Holy Spirit, who has guided me and instructed me, as always, in His most tender loving way.

Prologue

About Mum

My Mum, known as Dee, was a beautiful spirit-filled Christian lady. She was the type of person who always wanted to give to others. She always wanted to help those who found themselves in difficult circumstances, or genuinely just needed a kind word of encouragement.

She was the third child born to her mum and dad, but unfortunately the only child who lived. Her older brother (Kenneth) and sister (Doreen) both died in infancy and sadly she never knew them. However, as an only child, she grew up in a very loving home, doted on by her father.

She studied to become a nursery schoolteacher and thoroughly enjoyed all her years in education.

At the amazing age of eighty-eight, after suffering dementia for three years, she peacefully moved to Heaven.

Why is it in life that we always take for granted those who are dear and close to us; those who, with totally unselfish motives, continually give out and nourish us with their words of love and support? Yet now, as I look back upon the qualities that my mum showed and demonstrated on a day-to-day basis, I am so eternally grateful to have been blessed, taught and loved by such an amazing woman.

I do hope that this short account sets the scene, describing the kind of person that she was (and I feel still is, as you will see). As you read through this book, I know you will be able to share in this "glimpse into Heaven" through the perspective of her life as well as the things that Holy Spirit has "unveiled" to me.

Chapter One

The Entwining of Two Realms

Life is so short. As the Bible says, *"a day is as a thousand years"* Psalm 9:4. If only we could see each hour, each minute, each day as a valuable, irretrievable treasure walking through this life in preparation for eternity. Each spoken word, each expression of love and each act of kindness lives on into eternity. Each relationship, each incidental meeting is for a purpose and is intertwined into God's most amazing tapestry; threads and colours are woven into history throughout all generations.

Is it any wonder that each day can be as a thousand years? Each day has an infinite amount of consequences, words and acts of kindness that are far beyond our own finite imagination; each interacting in a huge labyrinth of expressions of love in this slice of time called "today".

I have come to see that this world is a dim shadow of the world to come. I have come to understand that Earth and Heaven are so much more interconnected, aligned and working in unison, than we could ever have imagined possible. Heaven is absolutely NOT an individual realm that works independently of the "here and now". It is actually interwoven into every minute, every word and every expression upon this Earth. The psalmist in Psalm 19:1-4 gives us an overwhelming illustration of the Heavens declaring the magnificence of our God together with the magnitude and force of the spoken word.

> *"The heavens declare the glory of God; and the firmament shows and proclaims His handiwork. Day after day pours forth speech, and night after night shows forth knowledge. There is no speech nor spoken word; their voice is not heard. Yet their voice goes out through all the Earth, their sayings to the end of the world."*

> Each relationship, each incidental meeting is for a purpose and is intertwined into God's most amazing tapestry; threads and colours woven into history throughout all generations.

These verses portray the invisible things of God, whose being is incontestably evident and whose glory shines brightly and unequalled throughout the Heavens. As He created ALL things by His spoken Word, the heavens, the skies and the Earth all resonate with the glory of their creator, which is representative of His handiwork. Just take a moment to ponder over how everything that exists bears the fingerprint of its creator.

I would like to draw your attention to this constant stream of communication "day after day pours forth speech". It is absolutely mind-blowing that speech (yes, even *our* speech) is part of a ceaseless voice, and that no spoken word is unheard or falls to the ground unnoticed. Words are containers or carriers of love, joy, peace, or conversely hate, jealousy or rage. As such, words are not empty but march on from the present where they are released into the fullness of all eternity.

So often, we get caught up with our "here and now" life on Earth, with the day-to-day routine of busyness within workplaces and families. Yet as we look beyond ourselves into the deeper purpose for which we have been placed on this planet, we can discover the part that we are playing in the destiny of all time. Yes, the destiny of all time - I appreciate this is a massive concept to consider: the orchestration of all of history; a huge stage of the interaction of all generations. As we contemplate this and our part in this, we may sometimes, in our own perspective, seem small and irrelevant in such a huge programme. Everyone has been fashioned and created in a unique way and placed in their own specific time in history to fulfil God's purpose and His plan. Every one of us has been given the gifts, the talents and abilities, the character and resources to carry out a portion of history; a piece in the "Jigsaw puzzle" of this slice of time. This "Master Plan" is of such grandeur and amazing magnificence that we should stand back in absolute awe of the God who created us and placed us here, in this moment of time, called "now". And yet despite the grandeur of this master plan God is overwhelmingly mindful of even the smallest detail of our lives. Every one of our cares, every one of our disappointments and every one of our achievements: He is intently aware of each moment and the outcome of every facet of our lives. Psalm 8:4 demonstrates this:

"What is man that you are mindful of him and the

> *son of man that you care for him? Yet you have made him but a little lower than God, and you have crowned him with glory and honor. You have made him to have dominion over the works of your hands;"*

What an awesome privilege and honour to be crowned with His glory, the same glory that the Heavens declare! When I read this psalm, I imagine David dipping into an angel's astonished exclamation as he considers God's handiwork in His creation of the being called "man". This Scripture appears to be a dialogue expressed from the angelic vantage point, with obvious awe and amazement. If you consider that the angelic force had seen Heaven in all of its glory, operating outside of time, then they observed the most monumental days of the first week on Earth. The first week of creation; the light, the waters, the earth, the vegetation, the living creatures, and then...And then the crowning glory, the masterpiece of all His creation...Man, who God made to have dominion over the works of His hands. Oh wow! how awesome, how magnificent! No wonder the angels were in awe and expressed their astonishment of His great creation.

Additionally, consider what the apostle Paul says in 1 Corinthians 2:6-10 about the significance God's people have ...

> *"Yet when we are among the full-grown (spiritually mature Christians who are ripe in understanding), we do impart a wisdom (the knowledge of the divine plan previously hidden); but it is indeed not a wisdom of this present age or of this world, nor of the leaders and rulers of this age, who are being brought to nothing and*

doomed to pass away."

Notice how Paul continues to say that we have God's own wisdom at our disposal in order to assist us in all our dealings upon this Earth - what a wonderful privilege that the angels are not privy to.

> *"But rather what we are setting forth is a wisdom of God once hidden and now revealed to us by God - (that wisdom) which God devised and decreed before the ages for our glorification (to lift us into the glory of His presence) but, on the contrary, ...What eye has not seen and ear has not heard and has not entered into the heart of man, God has prepared for those who love him (who hold Him in affectionate reverence, promptly obeying Him and gratefully recognizing the benefits He has bestowed).*
> *Yet to us God has unveiled and revealed them by and through His Spirit, for the (Holy) Spirit searches diligently, exploring and examining everything, even sounding the profound and bottomless things of God (the divine counsels and things hidden and beyond man's scrutiny)"*
> *1 Corinthians 2:6-10.*

As the Scripture above says, it is the job of Holy Spirit to unveil and reveal the profound and bottomless things of God to all His creation; to all those who have called upon His Name in order that we may be instrumental in carrying out our portion of His "Master Plan", which was God's original design for humanity.

God's heart is to reveal His unconditional love to us, in order to comfort us, in order to have relationship with us and in order to restore His precious creation. Everyone is overwhelmingly precious in His sight, yes, everyone! To give a glimpse into Heaven in order to show the workings of His plan and His love to all humanity is certainly on His agenda.

In our own natural mind and human capacity, we cannot fathom, grasp or understand the things of God, the things of the Spirit operating in the Earth realm nor even the things of our eventual heavenly home.

However, just considering two scriptures 2 Corinthians 5:17 and Colossians 1:10,

> "Therefore, if any person is [ingrafted] in Christ (the Messiah) he is a new creation (a new creature altogether); the old [previous moral and spiritual condition] has passed away."

> "And you are in Him, made full and having come to fullness of life you too are filled with the Godhead—Father, Son and Holy Spirit..."

Our born-again spirit is a new being where the literal Greek text says a "new species of being which never existed before". Additionally, in this new being the fullness of the Godhead dwells in bodily form...just think of that! Therefore, in our born-again capacity we *can* understand the realms of the spirit in all its dimensions in whatever way Holy Spirit reveals for our edification, instruction and growth. We can see revelations of Heaven and the world to come as Holy Spirit impresses these precious truths into our spirit.

It is our *spirit* that is made in the image of God. It is our spirit that communicates with the Father by the precious indwelling of Holy Spirit within us. We are made up of spirit, soul and body. It is our spirit that is in constant communication with Holy Spirit. It is out of our spirit that we can live and move and have our being. We must never underestimate the ability, the power and the wooing of Holy Spirit towards our hearts on a continual basis. This is entirely dependent on our own desire to grow deeper in our intimacy with the Father and the things of the spirit.

> To give a Glimpse into Heaven in order to show the workings of His plan and His love to all humanity is certainly on His agenda

Through caring for my mum during her illness, I realised the significance of a person's spirit. As we nurse and care for those who, for whatever reason, are about to depart from this Earth, we can be more aware of the life force within a person. At this time, we must not underestimate the supernatural power within a person's spirit. Even in times of great sickness, one's spirit is alive, active and totally responsive to its surroundings. It is only the body - the flesh - that dies. It is the spirit within each and every one of us that lives on into eternity.

Just two weeks before my mum's passing, I was so blessed to have first-hand experience of seeing her relate and communicate in a way that she had not been able to do for many years, due to the illness she had. It was almost as if the Lord enabled a window of time, maybe just seconds, on several occasions, when my mum expressed herself as she was before her illness with disarming clarity and purpose. As she spoke words of love and familiar family phrases that she had not voiced in years, as well as spiritual adoration, it so blessed my soul. It gave me direct confirmation that she was speaking things that came directly from her spirit by the inspiration of Holy Spirit. These words of communication are so very precious to me, for I know that the utterance came from the Spirit of God alone. I have heard of other people who have had similar experiences with their loved ones. How amazing to have absolute confirmation that her spirit was alive and that she had her inbound ticket reserved for Heaven. To be reminded that she was and would always be in the safekeeping of our Lord Jesus Christ - this is so very precious. The comfort of Holy Spirit is beyond all understanding, as He knows how to embrace us with eternal words of love. Keeping our eyes focused on Jesus and the communication that Holy Spirit has spoken directly into our spirit for our wellbeing is of paramount importance.

God's timing is always immaculate. I found that the timings and the intricate details of every day and hour leading up to my mum's departure from Earth were laden with inconceivable blessings of one form or another. As I walked through the final days with her, it was as if I was experiencing what the Scripture refers to in Isaiah 45:3, as being given "treasures in darkness" or "hidden riches of secret places". I was given so many treasures at this time that I felt materially and spiritually blessed, heavily laden with such revelation beyond anything I had ever imagined. I was overwhelmed in this season and could only express the whole experience of her passing away as "beautiful". All the orchestration of Holy Spirit and God's master plan in this one person's life entering

Heaven was simply "beautiful".

I so appreciated (and still do) the comfort of Holy Spirit, who transformed a season of mourning into joy unspeakable. I will portray these revelations and a glimpse of Heaven in a way that gives the reader an equal sense of being heavily laden with spiritually blessings and impressions beyond their imagination of the world to come.

Chapter Two

Love Transcends All Boundaries

It had been just under a week since my mum had moved to Heaven. I was simply sitting in my lounge in my favourite place, just listening and being open to the words of Holy Spirit, when I found myself peeking through into another world. Metaphorically speaking, it was as if I had been in a darkened room with the curtains fully closed, but as I drew near to open the curtains, the light streamed in, with rays far exceeding the brilliance of the noonday sun. These rays of light were of such magnitude, only limited by my inability to absorb their magnificence. Additionally, there was an overwhelming sense of peace; everything in order, an all-encompassing atmosphere of joy, but securely founded on love...everything orchestrated and, in its place, fashioned and created by the Creator of all things.

It was certainly as if I was only glimpsing into the heavenly realm, in my mind's eye, but I could sense an all-embracing atmosphere of Heaven invading my consciousness and the "here and now".

A Glimpse into Heaven

I want to explain the comfort that Holy Spirit gave me, instructing me, reassuring me and guiding me to an understanding of the events pertaining to my mum's entrance into Heaven.

I felt the awareness that angels came and escorted her to her new heavenly home. Love is the vehicle of Heaven. It is our love that embraces our dying loved one, as we whisper the most beautiful of earthly messages of love and farewell. Then love securely takes them by the hand, figuratively speaking, with a sense of "I don't want to let go," but a sense of "I need to let go." Then all of Heaven gets ready for an abundant entrance; all of Heaven rejoices as a soul finds victory over death and enters eternity with Him.

> I am absolutely convinced that words of love, expressed out of a heart full of love are the highest form of communication and will always live on in our memories, in our hearts and into eternity itself.

Love is the most powerful force in the whole universe, and love will carry every dying precious soul, moving into the realm of glory. Love will hold their hand right up until the entrance of Heaven. Love is the force that can let go, but also holds a person dear in one's heart, never to stop loving and cherishing.

It was Holy Spirit who spoke to me so tenderly, saying that I had held my mum's hand right up until the entrance of Heaven, as I passed her across the threshold and let go, and from there the Lord took her hand. She entered in, to reside for all eternity in the Everlasting.

Love Transcends All Boundaries

The day my mum left this Earth, I knew, without a shadow of a doubt, that she had "transcended" into Heaven. I was filled with the most unexplainable and totally abnormal joy. Granted, there was the relief that she was no longer suffering, but the knowledge that she had moved to Heaven was just so overwhelming, it consumed and overtook every emotion, every waking moment and every inner reflection. I always had a very close, intimate and sisterly relationship with my mum, but instead of a feeling that this had been severed, it felt as if it had actually been strengthened and empowered by the supernatural force of love.

I am absolutely convinced that words of love, expressed out of a heart full of love are the highest form of communication and will always live on in our memories, in our hearts and into eternity itself.

This almost new supernatural force of love was totally unconditional and was harnessed firmly in my innermost being in the place where my memories exist. The place of my memories could seemingly still release such pure love towards her. There was not a feeling of emptiness, but an overwhelming sense that the release of love would transcend all physical earthly boundaries. This was affirmed by Paul in 1 Corinthians 13:8 when he wrote,

> *"Love never fails (never fades out or becomes obsolete or comes to an end)."*

Just think and meditate on that …Love that never comes to an end!

Additionally, 1 John says:

"God is love"

The fabric of the whole universe is birthed out of and runs completely and exclusively in the Love of God.

It was a most bizarre time, when I could sense Heaven in the most tangible way. I could feel the closeness of the two realms, intermingled with life experiences.

I felt Holy Spirit educating and instructing me, showing me the workings of my mum's transition into Heaven.

I felt an all-embracing reassurance from the Lord: "we've got her, she is safe, she is complete, and she is with Me".

Oh, what joy filled my heart to know that my perfect Saviour had reached down and taken her by the hand and drawn her unto Himself, never again to feel pain, never again to be fearful or anxious. Oh, what a marvellous salvation, oh what an unexplainable gift of grace and mercy - such love.

Chapter Three

Love Overcomes All

Here, we are so accustomed to this Earth realm; we are so familiar with its workings and its dynamics and therefore our human understanding is conditioned to this realm. But when we move into the heavenly realm, we are initially completely unacquainted and unfamiliar with its workings and its dynamics.

The Scripture clearly illustrates this in 1 Corinthians 13:9-12:

> *"For our knowledge is fragmentary, incomplete and imperfect, and our prophecy/teaching is fragmentary, incomplete and imperfect. But when the complete and perfect comes, the incomplete and imperfect will vanish away (become antiquated, void, and superseded)"....*
>
> *"For now, we are looking in a mirror that gives only a dim, blurred reflection, but then when perfection comes, we shall see, in reality and face-to-face. Now I know in part, imperfectly, but*

then I shall know and understand fully and clearly, even in the same manner as I have been fully and clearly known and understood by God."

Holy Spirit showed me very clearly that because Christians are so accustomed to this world and unaccustomed to the world beyond, when a loved one leaves Earth and enters Heaven, they are sheltered and engulfed in love greater than they have ever experienced on this earth. This commences in the dying process at the time of passing, when there is a love that is so tender and all-powerful, which thunders to their aid, carrying them, encompassing them and surrounding the person to the very depths of every minute cell of their being, so that every care, pain and concern is simply absorbed by His love, never to be experienced again. This love causes every cell of their consciousness to resonate with a new and different melody: the melody of love. This force of love ensures that they are in no way overwhelmed by their new surroundings.

> Having those treasured moments of intimacy in our heart, pondering and reminiscing the beautiful, shared memories, is the true voice of love, occurring in a realm beyond our understanding.

Initially, a departed loved one clings, in their soul, more to the Earth realm and its customs and traditions, even though they are residing in Heaven. This is completely natural, and is an expected adjusting period, not to be rushed or hurried. If you consider that our soul has been impacted by words throughout the course of our lives, there is no wonder that there needs to be a de-cluttering process. There are words that have been spoken that are not profitable or edifying, but continue to resonate in the soul. It is in this transition period, which commences in Heaven, that each layer of the world's systems, beliefs and customs are, as it were, peeled away from the soul. It is as the soul embraces this force of love, allowing its full resonating power to have its complete work that the fullness of their redemption and their true being is revealed, unhindered by this world's old values, customs, and life experiences.

In our limited human understanding, our loved one, who has left Earth and entered Heaven is no longer with us, but because love transcends all understanding, the true dynamic of this transition is very different. Yes, we can know with every fibre of our being that they now reside in Heaven, but the truth is, (as I have already said) the realm of Heaven and the realm of Earth are actually very closely entwined. I'm certainly not saying that it is correct to attempt to contact those who have passed on, as it firmly states in Deuteronomy 18:11-12 that this is an abomination before the Almighty. However, the spirit realm in which love has its full expression has absolutely no bounds or finality, as demonstrated in 1 Corinthians 13:8.

> *"Love never fails, never fades out or becomes obsolete or comes to an end."*

There is therefore a place in the spirit realm where the power of love flowing from and to a loved one will never cease and will never end. This is a huge reassurance to all those who have lost dearly loved friends or family members... to have the assurance that they are thinking of you, just as you are thinking of them. Just think of that! There are times when you are centrally in their thoughts. Cherished memories are being recounted. Words are being expressed out of a heart that is now completely free of all the Earth's toils and trials. It is, however, incorrect to pray for the inhabitants of Heaven (they have no need of our prayers). A cherished thought or beautiful words wrapped in love will transcend the two realms. Having those treasured moments of intimacy in our heart, pondering and reminiscing the beautiful shared memories, is the true voice of love, occurring in a realm beyond our understanding. There are no limits for expressions of love; no limits, even between Earth and Heaven.

There is a period of time when the separation is still very new and raw for those on Earth. This is when the greatest comfort is manifested. The precious Holy Spirit will give comfort in the most amazing, unexpected and profound ways. After all Holy Spirit is known as the great comforter.

In Romans 1:27, it illustrates that the manifested presence of God has been made available to all men. During this particular time of grieving is when the spirit of God manifests the greatest demonstrations of comfort to both those who are children of God and those who are yet to be children of God. Through His power and His divinity, He is revealing Himself to those who mourn as the God who is love personified.

> *"for ever since the creation of the world, His invisible nature and attributes, that is, His eternal power and divinity, have been made intelligible and clearly discernible in and through the things that have been made (his handiworks)."*

There are countless instances where Holy Spirit repositions and comforts those who have been recently bereft. He is the true and only comforter. After all, the person of Holy Spirit has the title, amongst others, as the Comforter. We need therefore to allow His entrance into every aspect of this new season of our lives; a new season when a precious acquaintance is promoted to glory, and we find ourselves pondering the world to come. He can reveal to us amazing truths and visions as we permit Him to have full expression on the inside of our being. If you have lost someone dear, might I recommend that you take time to give Holy Spirit access into these memories and thoughts, allowing your spirit to soar with Him. As you do so your thoughts will collide with spiritual reality and earthly carnal thoughts will be replaced and superseded with visions, dreams and impressions from Heaven: a world that exists outside of time.

Although we are living in a fallen world, where the challenges and trials of this world are not God's original intention for His creation, we can choose to live our lives on Earth in the light of the important truths expressed in Ephesians 1:19-20. This is a truly overwhelming scripture that always leaves me pondering the greatness of our God and the enormity of what He has bestowed upon us.

> *"... And (so that you can know and understand) what is the immeasurable and unlimited and surpassing greatness of His power in and for us who believe, as demonstrated in the working of His mighty strength, which He exerted in Christ when He raised him from the dead and seated Him at His (own) right hand in the heavenly (places)"*

We have this power at work within us as we *choose to*

believe the promises in His Word. As the revelations contained in these pages impact your spirit, together with the understanding that we are filled with the fullness of God and have the very same power that raised Christ from the dead dwelling on the inside of us, my hope is that this glimpse into Heaven will turn into a greater revelation of what can be accomplished on this Earth. Although we cannot physically see the manifested glory of Heaven on a day-to-day basis in all its glorious splendour around us, we can certainly operate with an understanding of its existence, and therefore in faith by His grace bestowed towards us, see our lives moving in greater reality of His power.

Chapter Four

All of Heaven Anticipates

It had been just two weeks since my mum had moved to Heaven. I was reflecting upon all that had taken place over this period since she had gone. My attention turned to what it must have been like for those in Heaven anticipating her arrival; a time in Heaven, maybe a month or two before her passing, when attention of her imminent arrival was expected. It was as if the Holy Spirit was giving me a glimpse of the preparations that had taken place in Heaven prior to mum departing the Earth realm. I saw the following as I looked into the spirit. I had the feeling that some of these occurrences were directly associated with my mum but also that this is what happens on a regular basis for all believers who enter Heaven.

Oh, the bustle, such excitement and expectation reaching to that of almost fever pitch as a dear precious soul is awaited! Their arrival from the Earth realm is imminently expected and their relocation to their new heavenly abode is so very close. There is such fervent activity and energetic busyness as the finishing touches are put into place for their new heavenly home. There is no dust or dirt in Heaven, so the preparations, unlike on Earth, would not include cleaning! However, the highest attention to detail is very much sought to the ultimate level of perfection.

The scene I pictured, was one that was greater than any close family wedding, anniversary or birthday. There is no earthly celebration that can come close to such a glorious reunion. Friends and family with ardent delight, eagerness and excitement were scurrying around, ensuring that everyone was present, who should be there to greet and to bestow love and welcoming embraces upon their dearest loved one.

With shrieks of excitement, the atmosphere was charged with such a sense of eager expectation and glee. Each friend or relation had their own special greeting and their own special memories shared of a life on Earth. They were almost unable to contain their own excitement at this sweetest of reunions.

For some Heaven-bound individuals, their arrival has been long awaited. A husband or wife (who remained on Earth after the other and lived on for many years on Earth) has so sweet a reunion, with so much to express, share and recollect together. For others it has only been a short space of time; a life cut short or a child barely on Earth, returning to Heaven to continue to grow into adulthood. Consider also, those who have spent their whole life on Earth, praying for family members, only to depart this Earth with their prayers seemingly unfulfilled. But now they are welcoming the one they diligently prayed for; year in and year out, and at last they see the fulfilment of their prayers, manifesting and coming to fruition as they learn that their loved one has indeed later received Jesus as Saviour. What excitement; what a jubilant party, comes upon hearing this news. All of Heaven rejoices! This eventual heavenly reunion is beyond our human understanding and is so very, very sweet, as the tears of joy stream abundantly down their faces to be wiped away in a moment of sheer excitement as they come home.

In 2 Peter 1:11 it states,

> *"You will receive a rich welcome into the eternal Kingdom of our Lord and Saviour Jesus Christ."*

Our welcome is far more than just an entrance into Heaven, but into His eternal Kingdom. The only way to enter is through Him, for He is the Way, the Truth and the Life. It is only through Him. It clarifies this in Hebrews 10:19,

> *"We have boldness to enter into the holiest by the blood of Jesus...A new and living way."*

So, this is a blood-bought entrance! As Jesus said, there is joy in Heaven over one sinner who repents. There is overwhelming joy in Heaven over a forgiven sinner coming home to glory.

We have no idea of the people whose lives we have impacted during the course of our life on Earth - folks who will want to be present at our arrival into His Kingdom. There will be those we have loved unconditionally, encouraged unreservedly or there may even be a stranger with whom we have shed a tear or those whose spirit has been lifted as we have shared a passing smile. This is illustrated so conclusively in Matthew 25:40 where Jesus says,

A Glimpse into Heaven

> *"the King will reply to them, truly I tell you, insofar, as you did it for one of the least of my these my brethren, you did it for me."*

Oh! how amazing to be greeted by those whose lives we have touched in some positive way on this Earth. What a privilege to be counted as instrumental in their own life's journey and to be joyfully reunited.

Chapter Five

Arrived Home Safely!

Arrivals!! Just like the arrival section of an airport, but immensely more controlled, peaceful and beautiful, here was the arrivals portal for those transitioning to glory. Welcoming throngs of excited family and friends were ready to greet those entering in through what we commonly call "the pearly gates".

The euphoria was overwhelming: the sense of delight and sheer excitement and relief was beyond human understanding. So often we have used the phrase "abundant entrance", oh! how it is just that - abundant in every sense of the word. The atmosphere was charged with electrifying excitement with a sense of tangible anticipation. All Heaven rejoices!

> The eruption turned into harmonious praise interspersed with shouts of adoration to Him who had bought her home

I will now explain the first two weeks of adjustment in Heaven, as the Holy Spirit tenderly kept me informed of how mum was doing and what she was up to - it seemed almost bizarre, but I understand now that love has no boundaries. He was tenderly illustrating to me that after so many years of looking after mum, He (the great physician) was more than able to take care of her and I could relax, knowing she was safe. For those who were ready to embrace their new life in Heaven, the adjustment period was swift and progressive. Help was at hand every step of the way, to progress to total inclusion and familiarity with the ways of the operation of the Kingdom of Heaven; fully understanding and conversant with its customs. My mum has always been trusting, accommodating and eager to learn and she was particularly interested in the workings of the spirit realm, so I would imagine her period of acclimatisation was relatively swift.

I asked Holy Spirit to show me a glimpse of the transition experience. He made it clear that we are first and foremost spirit beings created in the image of God, and as such our spirit is always awake and in tune with its surroundings. No matter what terrible disease or affliction someone goes through, the spirit is always alert, awake and ready to hear the voice of the Word, their Saviour, the Lord Jesus Christ. Therefore, everyone is fully conscious of the transition experience from the Earth realm to the Heaven realm.

The first thing that I learnt was that a person would be completely engulfed and encompassed with a sense of peace: peace beyond human understanding, almost more than a soul could bear. Every earthly fear, concern or worry would vanish away. Then overwhelming waves of liquid love, beyond the most extreme love that we have ever received or given on this Earth, would permeate every cell of our being, infusing us with an inner joy totally unearned, unconditional and yet fully tangible.

"To be wrapped in His loving embrace and to be encircled by the power of His love..."

Oh, such great salvation, oh what a mystery and oh what a magnificent Saviour!

Praise God for such an awesome salvation. We really only know in part the phenomenal sacrifice, which was made by God our Father. His love for us is completely unconditional, completely selfless and all-encompassing. He is the Alpha; He is the Omega. Truly from the beginning to the very end, He is everything. As we glimpse into the heavenly realm, it is then that our perspective increases, and the panoramic view of our understanding broadens.

Thank you, thank you, thank you, heavenly Father for everything....

I suddenly heard a monumental gargantuan eruption, as a host of bystanders shrieked with excitement; "Look, look! She's there, that's her dear little face, she is here now. Come, come let's run to her. Let's embrace her. Oh, I'm so excited that she is finally with us. She is finally safe. Praise Him, for bringing her home to us; for revealing His great salvation to her. Precious Lamb of God." The eruption turned into harmonious praise interspersed with shouts of adoration to Him who had bought her home.

Food is a part of the welcoming process. This seemed a bit strange to me, initially, but as I questioned the Holy Spirit, I was reminded that during or after many miracles that Jesus performed and during many other instances, Jesus would say "Get the people something to eat". But why? Food and nourishment are a part of our well-being. A baby will always sleep better when its tummy is full. Likewise, we are more at rest and more content and satisfied when we have taken in good nourishment. Jesus also referred to the Word of God as spiritual nourishment, so there is a suitable correlation.

Platters of the most exquisite, nutritious, delightful morsels were available for all to share at Heaven's entrance. The fruit was so luscious and bursting with flavour and juice. It was as if the fruit was completely saturated in its own juice, and a small bite released a torrent of mouth-watering juice of every description and aroma. This refreshing liquid drenched the very inner parts of the being. There were dainty truffle-like wafers, flavoured with everything imaginable. Tasty bites of all shapes and sizes, colours, hues and aromas filled the platters. I could only liken this to dainty food or hors d'oeuvres served at the commencement of a huge celebration, party or banquet. What a most amazing experience, a feast in any earthly perspective, but not in Heaven, for this was just a foretaste and appetiser for the purpose of refreshing those wearied from their earthly journey, and specifically to unite and welcome family and friends together after times of separation.

Throughout the Heavens, the atmosphere and the skies were ringing with choruses and praise; an abundant crescendo of the most harmonious, electrifying worship rang through the atmosphere, so that every living being and every plant harmoniously entered into and was surrounded by the worship of the one phenomenal King of Kings and Lord of Lords.

This reminded me of when Jesus was on Earth in Luke 19:36,40 when He proclaimed that even nature would cry out in praise,

> "...and as He rode along, the people kept spreading their garments on the road. As He was approaching the city, at the descent of the Mount of Olives, the whole crowd of the disciples began to rejoice and to praise God (extolling Him exultantly and) loudly for all the mighty miracles and works of power that they had witnessed. Crying, blessed (celebrated with praises) is the King who comes in the name of the Lord! Peace in Heaven (freedom there from all of the distresses that are experienced as the result of sin) and glory (majesty and splendour) in the highest (heaven)"... "I tell you that if these keep silent, the very stones will cry out."

In Heaven, there is absolutely no restriction upon praise as there is on Earth; everything is harmoniously aligned, created for and infused with praise. It is the very breath of Heaven, the very rhythm of Heaven, creating its ambience and very expression of Heaven.

Oh! how our praise and worship of the King of Kings and Lord of Lords upon the Earth is such a minute expression of what we are capable of, of what we were created to be; He is so very worthy! If only we could fling away our inhibitions, self-consciousness and the cares that hold us back, and truly be what He has created us to be. "To be lost in wonder, adoration and praise."

He is so worthy!

A Glimpse into Heaven

I took a further glimpse into the Heavens, into a place in the spirit where I seemed to be able to visit repeatedly in order to hear the dialogue of the spirit.

I began to hear a new conversation between my mum (Dee) and her sister, Doreen. (As I wrote in the prologue my mum's sister died when she was only a few weeks old and therefore my mum, being the younger sister, had never met her).

"Dee, Dee, it's me Doreen, I'm your big sister who you have never met, come, come dearest Dee, let me embrace you to myself, let me hold you in my arms, it has been such a very long time that I have been longing to meet you. Welcome, welcome! I am so much looking forward to spending time together, getting to know one another and showing you around. Oh, look how alike we are! I can't wait to find out all about you, what you like and what you enjoy and to do all those sisterly things together! I also want to fully understand what it was like on the Earth and all the things you accomplished during the years you spent there. You must give me a full account of my relatives that remain there for I am also longing one day to meet them too." Dee looked on amazed but content as her sister continued. "But first, Dee, let me show you your new home, so that you can take a little rest, as we do not want to overwhelm you. There will be plenty of time to meet all those people who were here to welcome you. But first you must rest a while."

Chapter Six

Adventures in Heaven

During the first two weeks after my mum had moved on, I had an impression of what she was doing and the surroundings around about her. I was in church at the time, in a normal Sunday morning service when in my mind's eye, I saw her sitting upon a huge smooth stone at the water's edge. As far as the eye could see, was a huge glistening lake or maybe a sea, so peaceful and yet bubbling with life. The radiance with which the lake glistened with every colour imaginable was immensely beautiful and yet the waters were totally transparent. To one side of her was a tree with the most exquisite blossom and hanging branches over the lake. It was a glorious day.

My mum was looking serene, peaceful and immensely content just sitting looking towards the waters. She was no longer the age that she was when she had left the Earth realm, but she was in her late 20s or early 30s. I immediately recognised her. She was dressed in summer attire; a summer dress with floral print which would have been in keeping with the fashion on Earth at her age. She was beautiful, and she shone with such a radiance. The smile upon her face portrayed a huge sense of being totally at rest. She seemed to be alone as she gazed upon the beauty before her, but there was never a sense of her being alone, but instead she seemed to be engulfed by the serenity and tranquillity of the moment in total peacefulness.

Later that day I took some time out to revisit this picture

that I had received of my mum and to ask Holy Spirit some further questions.

I asked Him, "What is she doing? What has she been doing?"

To these questions, I was astounded to get these most detailed precious replies impressed into my spirit.

"She is sitting by the waters of restoration. These are the most incredibly restoring and calming waters. They are full of everything that is needed for the restoring of the soul, after all the Earth realm's experiences."

I replied, "So how does this happen?"

"These are the waters of life, infusing life into the innermost being. They will penetrate to the very heart and soul. They are not painful. They are immensely soothing and immensely refreshing. One dip into the water is sufficient to start the healing process, the restoration process and an invigorating process… bathing away all of the cares, frustrations, and hurts that have influenced the soul realm from years spent upon the Earth. All those who enter into their new heavenly abode spend a period of time in these waters. For those who have spent a long time in the Earth realm and have experienced many difficulties, they spend longer, allowing this restoration process to wash away all of their cares, unhappiness, earthly difficulties and negative impressions that have molded their souls during years on Earth. However, those who have experienced fewer difficulties or been on Earth for a shorter period of time don't necessarily spend so much time in these waters.

Every precious soul in Heaven is known intimately by the Father, and as such no one is pressured into doing something that they are uncomfortable with. It is, however, good to be teachable and accommodating to the Spirit of God, who will restore and build one's soul. This quality is looked upon greatly in the Kingdom of Heaven. However, there are those who, for whatever reason, or for whatever experience that they have been through on this earthly realm, may feel unworthy or totally overwhelmed by this process of transformation before them, and that is fine. Nobody is forced to do anything.

However, there is absolute restoration to complete wholeness available to all through these waters."

Holy Spirit continued to expound the answers to my questions. One of the funniest things He said was, "She has only been here for less than an Earth week, and she has changed her hairstyle three times." I just love the way Holy Spirit gives us the reassurance and sometimes intimate details in such a loving and reassuring manner...things that are dear to us, but somewhat irrelevant to others. The impression I received was "she's tried this, and she's tried that and she's happy now."

"She has also been spending time with friends who she knew on Earth." I was hugely surprised to learn that she was talking with her friends. For some unknown reason, I had a very unrealistic impression that people in Heaven possibly floated around on clouds, devoid of communication with one another. But in reality, those loved ones who have already gone on ahead of us often talk with such fondness about those who are still on Earth. They recall memories and character traits with such tenderness, laughing and enjoying shared memories on

Earth and eagerly awaiting the sweetest of reunions of an eventual homecoming. I had been very ignorant!

When I asked Holy Spirit, what mum was talking about with her friends I was astonished and very emotional when I received His reply. "Your mum's been bragging about you...she's so very proud of you." Wow, what comfort to know that although they are living in a realm where we cannot have access to them, we are very much in their thoughts and conversations on a regular basis. Just think on that and allow Holy Spirit to minister such comfort and revelation to you if you have lost someone dear.

> ...before the spirit of the new baby left Heaven for his Earth-bound journey, he had been tenderly kissed by his grandma, who was in Heaven, sending him on his way from Heaven to embark upon his earthly journey.

Under no circumstances are those who have gone before us denied, disadvantaged or prevented from celebrating the events on Earth that appertain to their loved ones. For instance, a wedding, a birth or a salvation are equally anticipated with such excitement and celebrations in Heaven.

On a separate occasion, I received a glimpse into the heavenly activities as a young couple on Earth who were about to have a baby, had recently lost one of their own parents. Holy Spirit impressed upon me that before the spirit of the new baby left Heaven for his Earth-bound journey, he had been tenderly kissed by his grandma, who was in Heaven, sending him on his way from Heaven to embark upon his earthly journey. Do not ever think that these two realms operate independently. God is love, and as such there can never be division between those who operate in love. Love is the most uniting and fundamental force in this whole universe.

Chapter Seven

Heavenly Home

The Holy Spirit went on to tell me a little bit about my mum's house in Heaven. The Bible tells us in Proverbs 24:3 – 4 how our homes on Earth are to be built and decorated,

> *"Through skilful and godly wisdom is a house (a life, a home, family) built, and by understanding it is established (on a sound and good foundation), and by knowledge shall its chambers (of every area) be filled with all precious and pleasant riches."*

It makes me wonder how much more will our heavenly houses be adorned. Additionally, in this Scripture, it refers to the home being so much more than just rooms in a structural building but instead it resembles a life, a family, and our relationships, hence reflecting all that we hold dear.

Whilst out walking one day, minding my own business, not thinking of anything much in particular, I came across a group of town houses. Suddenly I felt overwhelmed as I gazed at these buildings. I shut my eyes and allowed Holy Spirit to talk to me in a way I had by now become accustomed to. I felt I had been looking at a house very similar to my mum's new house and Holy Spirit was wanting to give me a glimpse of her new abode in Heaven. I saw a picture of my mum's house, in my mind's eye: a three-storey sort of townhouse. I questioned Holy Spirit, asking why it was a townhouse instead of a large mansion or country abode, as I had always been led to believe extravagance was not an issue whatsoever in Heaven; so, this seemed somewhat modest. The answer I received was that, when my mum was first married she lived in a townhouse and this was one of her happiest times on Earth.

The outside of the townhouse was very sturdy-looking. It didn't have any particularly ornate architecture, but it was still a handsome-looking house. However, as I took a glimpse on the inside of this relatively simple house, it became so much more elaborate and individually styled to suit her taste. I was overwhelmed with the fragrances that permeated the house. Peaches and cream - such a strong sweet aroma filled the house - interspersed with wafts of freshly baked cookies. As I took a look around, many corners of the house had vase-like features built into its ornate architecture. Instead of there being cut flowers, in these vases, there were living flowers growing from within the very fabric of vase-like structures in the house. Each corner was therefore filled with the most beautiful flowers of every different colour, description and fragrance.

In the hall, there was a half oval table, and upon this table, there was a tower of boxes. Each box was beautifully decorated with matching ribbons and bows. There were boxes of all shapes and sizes, all most lavishly adorned. I wondered initially what was in these boxes and what was the purpose of them being in the hallway. But I was then taken back to an earlier conversation about the abundant entrance into Heaven, so I would suppose these were welcoming gifts from those wanting to show their love and appreciation.

As I mounted the stairs, the banister rail was intertwined with the most beautiful rose-like shrub. No thorns, just beauty, elegance and the most overwhelming of fragrances. This was not really a surprise to me, as mum had thoroughly enjoyed flowers, shrubs, and blooms of any kind whilst on Earth.

As I mounted the stairs, I could hear shrieks of laughter coming from the upper floor, but I shall leave this to later in the chapter.

The first floor contained the most spacious lounge with huge patio-like doors onto a massive balcony which in turn had steps into the garden area. From the balcony, all three sides of the garden could be seen. The panoramic view of the garden was simply spectacular: the garden seemed to embrace the balcony with trailing shrubs, plants and wall flowers of every description.

There were the most ornate pergolas, gazebos, with shrubs cascading and growing in every direction from within them and entwining around the beautifully carved pillars and posts of these most magnificent structures. There were paths throughout the garden weaving through the flowerbeds. The flowerbeds were filled with flowers of every colour, shape and fragrance beyond imagination;

the hue of colours throughout the garden was far beyond the spectrum of colours on Earth. Not only were the shrubs and flowers far more exotic than here on Earth, but they were also making melody amongst themselves; a background sound in perfect harmony that blended unobtrusively into the whole ambience of the garden. The flowers, all in bloom, were dancing and shimmering in the gentle breeze, as if they had their own individual melody that they were moving to. All these flowers seem to radiate life, like nothing I have ever seen.

The Scripture came to mind in Psalm 150:6, where is says,

> *"Let everything that has breath and every breath of life praise the Lord"*

There were areas of grass, sculpted and intermingled in pockets throughout the garden. The grass was lush and was as if each blade had been perfectly manicured and set-in place to provide a soft magnificent carpet of greenery. Everything - every flower, every leaf and every branch seemed to be set in its perfect position and yet moved in harmony to create further scenic positions.

Every so often, from beyond the garden, I could hear various groups of people singing praises to God as they passed along to their destination. Each voice had a melody in its own right, which was in total harmony and seemed as if all of Heaven joined in to make an overwhelming orchestra of praise. All the flowers turned their heads towards this melody. As everything within the sound of the praise joined in, this created a huge crescendo of adoration which engulfed everything in its wake into an overwhelming superabundant reverence of praise, glorifying the King of Kings and Lord of Lords. And the exuberance and expression of life was beyond anything I could understand.

Every turn of the path gave a completely new vista and perspective of the garden. The trees were all full of life: full of leaves, full of blossom and full of fruit. I have never even imagined fruit of such extravagance. These fruits were all ripe, exotic and bursting with juice. I noted a hanging fruit that was oozing and dripping with a sweet syrup-like substance.

Another turn of the path revealed the most beautiful pond and waterfall; flowers and greenery adorned the sides of the water. The water rushing down the waterfall was bubbling with such life as it cascaded from one level to another. The spray from these ripples seemed hugely refreshing, not wet, but invigorating.

I turned back towards the house, after taking a last look at the garden. I returned to the upper floor where I had heard such excitement, and as I peeked into the room, I could see about half a dozen young children around a baby grand piano. They were having a whale of a time, singing and playing. Others were running in and out of the room shrieking with laughter, absorbed in some unknown game.

"Who are these children?" I enquired.

"These are children without any mummies and daddies in Heaven. Your mum has truly found her vocation. She is such a blessing to each and every one of these children. She is devoted to their happiness, to their well-being and to their development. Some of these children will one day be united with family members, but until then, she is looking after them and caring for them as her own. No

A Glimpse into Heaven

child in Heaven is ever left on their own to fend for themselves, but instead they are cared for with every bit of tenderness and loving-kindness that can be bestowed upon them.

Chapter Eight

Children were not Created to Suffer

So why are there children in Heaven? You might well ask. How are they taken care of without a parent or family member? How can it be better for the child to grow up without a parent?

Children are an integral part of Heaven, being fully conversant with their surroundings, and the situation and circumstances that has brought them into Heaven.

All those on Earth who have departed at an early age or as an unborn babe will go straight to Heaven to be looked after in the most attentive and perfect way possible. They lack nothing, and yet, they are not self-centred. They learn the mighty truths of the Kingdom of Heaven, but they are not conceited or arrogant. They have such love bestowed upon them by an awesome and affectionate heavenly Father, and grow up with wisdom and understanding beyond their childhood age.

Having said this, I must just point out that it is never, ever, ever, God's will to see a child suffer, or a child or unborn baby die at any age. But just saying that it is not the will of God, does not mean that it does not happen. I would like to dispel the myth that God needs "a child to be an angel in Heaven." God does not lack angels in order that a child must be taken from the Earth to fulfil this purpose in Heaven, with all the resultant suffering and loss. This is not God.

It is important to understand that God has made man in His own image. Angels are not the same as human beings but have their own specific purpose in Heaven and on the Earth. The Scripture clearly states in Genesis 1:27

> *"God created man in His own image, in the image and likeness of God He created him; male and female He created them."*

Even though angels and human beings are both choice-making beings, God has given dominion of the Earth to man, not to angels. Angels have their own specific tasks assigned to them, including watching over those who are heirs of salvation. David re-iterates this in Psalm 8:4 when it says,

> *"What is man that you are mindful of him, and the son of (earth born) man that you care for him? Yet you have made him, but a little lower than God, and you have crowned him with glory and honour. You have made him to have dominion over the works of your hands; you have put all things under his feet."*

These Scriptures clearly define the status with which God

has created us. The awesomeness and magnificence with which He has fashioned us to be in His own image is frankly beyond human understanding, but not beyond the understanding of the spirit realm in which we live and move and have our being. We have also been recreated, in Christ, to have authority over all things in the sphere of our operation upon this Earth.

The difference that sets us apart from other created beings is that we are a spirit being that joins with our body and soul to make us a unique three-part being.

God created Adam (mankind), to meet His desire for communion and companionship. Likewise, we have been created to have the ability to reproduce after our own kind, DNA and character to satisfy our need for companionship and relationship.

Children are unquestionably a gift of God. As the Bible says a man is blessed who has a quiver of many children in Psalm 127:3

> *"Behold, children are a heritage from the Lord, the fruit of the womb, a reward. As arrows are in the hand of a warrior, so are the children of one's youth."*

Therefore, there is no way that a loving God would contradict himself, in order that it would be His will for a child to suffer. In suffering, there is no learning experience that is designed for our betterment. Suffering was never part of God's design, it only came about after the fall.

Prior to the fall, Adam met with God on a regular basis in

the cool of the day to walk, talk and enjoy fellowship with His Father. This can be seen in Genesis 3:8. Can you imagine, what they spoke about...how God explained, taught & nurtured Adam; the crown of His creation, bestowing upon him a magnitude of wisdom and knowledge, undergirded in love? Maybe day after day, He showed him greater wonders in His creation. After all, it was God who brought each one of the multitudes of the varieties of animals, birds and reptiles to Adam, for him to proclaim a name upon each one of them. Surely this would not have been a few short hours of declaring, I call this 'a giraffe', I think this should be 'an elephant', I call this 'a tiger' and so forth, but an education of such wonderment as Adam was given massive insights into God's magnificent creation. Just think of the information He would have imparted to Adam at this time and explanations of the functions and abilities of each species presented to him.

We have not comprehended the depths of the fullness of the relationship God desires to have with us. The best parent/child relationship upon this Earth has not even come close to the unconditional relationship of love that God wants to have with each and every one of us.

The relationship between a parent and a child was created to mimic the relationship God originally intended to have with Adam - this was the same relationship that was created to be experienced between God and all humanity. This is the very essence of civilisation and relationships at their very core, and in fact the essence of love itself. It is the kind of communion that a loving father aspires to nurture and encourage towards a child. We gain so much insight into how our heavenly Father desires that we communicate and interact with Him from watching how a child interacts with a parent that they have come to trust. As we observe a child's good or bad behaviour towards an adult, we can often see a resemblance in our own behaviour towards our heavenly Father! Sometimes we can be reminded of how we should, as adults, completely trust and communicate with God; our Father. It is us, adults, who need to become more childlike in our relationship with our heavenly Father, just as it says in Matthew 18:3

> *"whoever will humble himself therefore and become like this little child (trusting, lowly, loving, forgiving) is greatest in the kingdom of heaven."*

As a parent has such unconditional love for their child, and would, in certain circumstances want to bear the pain or suffering a child is experiencing, in order that the child does not need to suffer; so much more, our heavenly Father, cannot bear to see suffering.

We must firmly understand that we live in a world that is subject to the curse and fallen humanity. Everyone born into this Earth is of the Adamic race and has sinned and fallen short of the glory of God. Everyone needs a Saviour; the sinless Lamb of God, who has paid the full price for every wrongdoing and taken the full price of every suffering, disease and ultimately our death. It is only through our acknowledgement of Him, the Lord Jesus Christ, that we can be made spotless, as if we had never sinned, and be called righteous in Him.

Suffering has therefore come as a result of sin upon the Earth. It is never directly measured towards a particular sin, but it is part of the Earth-cursed system. There is no exemption for a child any more than an adult. But obviously seeing a child suffer is devastating for the loving family involved.

Let us turn our attention now to the activities of Heaven and to the children who reside there. I have learnt so much information by revelation from the Holy Spirit.

Children are very precious in the sight of God. Children are incredibly resilient and are often able to bear and walk through the worst of circumstances with an inner grace that astounds us all.

Just as Jesus, on the Mount of Olives, was met by Moses and Elijah, and strengthened for the ordeal He was to go through, we are given angels for our benefit, who work for those who are heirs of salvation. As it says in Hebrews 1:14:

> *"...are not the angels, all ministering spirits (servants) sent out in service (of God for the assistance) of those who are to inherit salvation?"*

I have been privileged to witness three different occurrences of how angels were sent to protect, encourage and walk with me in particular circumstances. How much more are the angelic hosts available to minister to children, to strengthen them and to walk with them. In Matthew 18:10 Jesus teaches that we should not "despise these little ones", (referring to the children) and goes on to say:

> *"...for I tell you that in Heaven their angels always are in the presence of, and look upon the face of my Father, who is in Heaven."*

Is this not remarkable? Why would an angel who has been assigned to a particular child be always in the presence of and be looking upon God's face? Does this not portray the huge price; the huge importance God places upon the admonition and instruction of these little ones? God wants all to be saved and come to the knowledge of the truth, so it is imperative that early guidance is of utmost importance. It makes absolute sense that He would want every child to be given the best possible start in life at an early age. In Proverbs 22:6 the Bible illustrates this:

> *"Train up a child in the way he should go and when he is old, he will not depart from it."*

As I have already said, all "baby" spirits, created in the image of God, and out of God, originate in Heaven and are sent to inhabit a new created life on Earth. All humanity has originated in Heaven. Babies and young children are more accustomed to spiritual activity. They are more receptive to the things of the spirit at an early age because they have spent less time, to date, in the Earth realm. It is as a child grows, that his familiarity with the spirit realm diminishes unless his parents bring him up in constant union with the ways of the spirit.

Every childhood soul is invaluable in the sight of God. Do not underestimate the worth that our heavenly Father places on every child's life. Every seed created in the earthly realm is of immense importance to God. If Jesus had had to die for one person; one person in all of humanity, He would have paid that price.

If only we could see…not in a 'mirror dimly', but with all the radiance and brilliance and magnificence of the operation of the angelic hosts as they carry out Father's orders upon this Earth.

If only we could see…the tenderness with which the mighty Holy Spirit of God works in unison with the Word and the person of the Lord Jesus Christ.

If only we could see…the full assembly of the workings of Heaven, as a sickly dying child is tenderly, carefully embraced and carried to Heaven. What a sight this would be, what an overwhelming panoramic understanding we would have of the immense, unconditional, overwhelming love our Father has bestowed upon us. There is no limit to His love. But for now, we must follow what it says in John 20:29

> *"Jesus said to Thomas, 'Because you have seen me, Thomas, do you now believe?' Blessed and happy and to be envied are those who have never seen me and yet have believed and adhered to and trusted and relied upon me."*

There is a huge place of revelation available in the spirit realm for those who are prepared to take this verse literally, and to fall into the loving arms of our Father, believing Him for greater understanding - beyond the natural human understanding - for a precious loved one who no longer resides with us. God does not want to keep from us the revelation of Heaven; nor of our loved ones who reside there. He wants to pour His Spirit of revelation out in these days and in these hours; revelation of the loving Father that He truly is, in order for our comfort and understanding.

God our Father fully appreciates the pain, the sorrow, the tearing and the parting when a precious child is taken from us. He hears the questions that we naturally have. He understands the void and emptiness that our soul feels. He feels the bewilderment and agony as our soul longs for it to have been different. But He is compassion himself.

When Lazarus was found to be dead for a period of three days, and although Jesus knew that He was about to raise him from the dead, He was still moved with compassion and He wept with those He loved as they displayed their grief. How bizarre is it that when He was about to do a phenomenal miracle of raising His friend from the dead, He responded in love to those He loved and was overwhelmed with their display of sorrow? Do not underestimate how much God sees the agony and overwhelming grief that parents endure at times. But He has provided a comforter (in the person of Holy Spirit) to give supernatural comfort to arrest the natural and bring us to a higher place in Him. Where in Him, we can truly say, I have no understanding now, but I have the peace that surpasses my understanding. I have a joy that comes from within that is unexplainable. It can only be and has to be from the spirit realm.

> God our Father fully appreciates the pain, the tearing, the sorrow and the parting when a precious child is taken from us.

Do not forget that it was the Father, when His son was on the cross, who had to "turn the lights out" to make darkness, hide the shame at noon day and who "turned His face away", as He could no longer bear the sight. Mark 15:33 says, *"and when the sixth hour (about midday) had come, there was darkness over the whole land until the ninth hour (about 3 o'clock). And at the ninth hour Jesus cried with a loud voice, Eloi, Eloi, lama sabachthani? - Which means, my God, my God, why have you forsaken me (deserting me and leaving me helpless and abandoned)?"*

He fully appreciates.

He fully understands.

And He fully wants to comfort every grieving heart.

Chapter Nine

Infants in Heaven

I am convinced that every aborted, miscarried or a stillborn baby upon death will go directly to Heaven. These children were never in a place to call upon a most marvellous Saviour, and therefore return to Heaven, from where they came.

I was just pondering how a pre-term baby would be looked after in Heaven, when I saw a picture in the realm of the spirit and what was seemingly an answer to my question. I saw a very brightly lit room where these tiny lives were being nurtured, loved, protected and grew into infancy. It was a most bizarre picture of hundreds of white oval-like "pods" about two feet in length by one foot. These pods were supported at waist height by a central leg to the ground. Would I call this a large nursery room? Yes,

> There seemed to be times when each angel used their wings to carefully cover the top of the pod to seemingly deflect the strength of the light for a certain period of time.

maybe. The light in this room was far brighter and shone with an intensity that seemed to suggest that a life force streamed from every particle of this light which descended upon these pods. I felt that this light force was stronger than anywhere else in the Heavens. It was specifically created to fashion, mold and develop the precious life forces that had not grown into maturity on the Earth. In the centre of each one of these pods was a tiny, tiny being. Some not yet resembling a baby but were a pinkish blob with a pulsating bright red centre whilst others were further developed, and their tiny form could be depicted. Every single one, however, was pulsating with a strong and uniform heartbeat. There was an angel guarding and watching over each pod. These angels were intently focused on the tiny life force that they were guarding. There seemed to be times when each angel used their wings to carefully cover the top of the pod to seemingly deflect the strength of the light for a certain period of time. I can only liken this room to that of an intensive care ward, but there was no commotion, there was no communication and no busyness. There was a tranquil and peaceful ambience of Heaven residing in and permeating the atmosphere. This was all I saw of these tiny lives.

The question I asked Holy Spirit next was: "So do all children grow into adulthood in Heaven, prior to their family members joining them there?"

There was no generalisation to the answer I received. (For again, nothing is rushed in Heaven; nothing is done that would compromise the desires or well-being of the families involved, even if the families are still in the Earth realm.)

Infants in Heaven

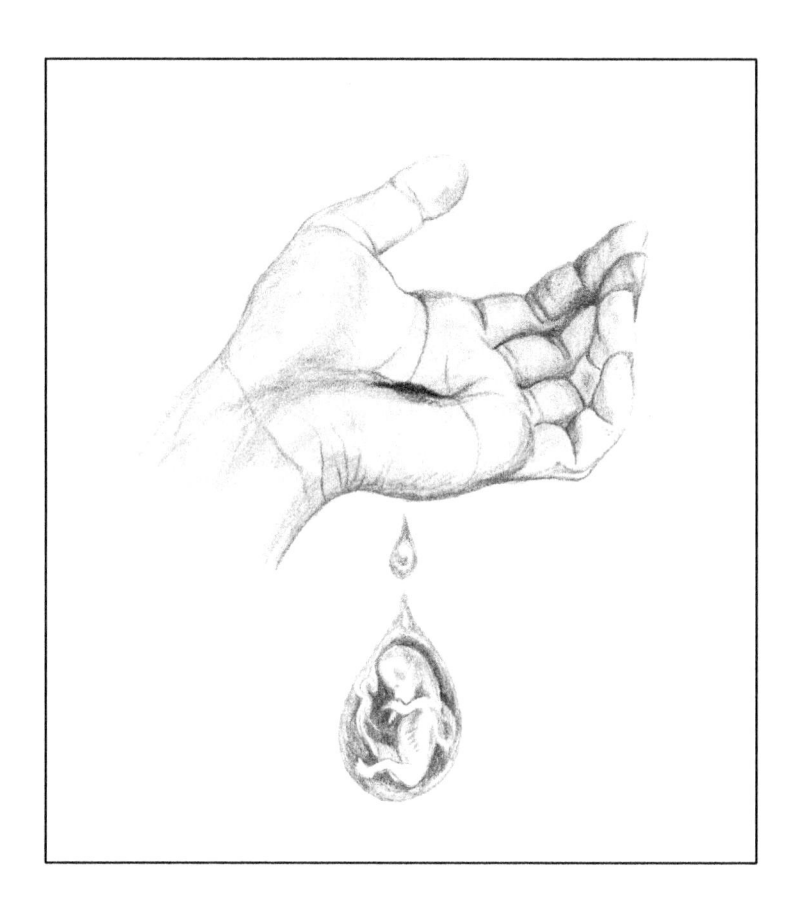

His blood paid the full price so that every aborted, miscarried baby and every child who dies prematurely is made complete and returns to Heaven.

Holy Spirit said that for those Christian families who have lost unborn children, for whatever reason, or lost infants, it might well be that the child does not grow into adulthood but remains the child that the family so desperately and longingly desired. The child waits in this safe and secure place, not disadvantaged or frustrated in any way, to grow into adulthood nurtured by the parents once their time on Earth is completed. Others grow into adulthood to eagerly await the homecoming of the families. There are no set rules. Everything is done in love and for the utmost consideration of the families involved.

Other infants may never be united with their natural earthly families because their families refused to accept the salvation message. However, there are also Christians on Earth who have never been able to fulfil the desire to have children and as, the Scripture says in Galatians 4:27,

> "for it is written in the Scriptures, rejoice, O barren woman, who has not given birth to children; break forth into joyful shout, you who are not feeling birth pangs, for the desolate woman has many more children than she who has a husband."

There is a huge programme of activities that children undertake in Heaven; not only being taught the ways of the kingdom of God and the information about their families upon the Earth, but also activities that are beyond our understanding. Yes, of course, there is fun and laughter; there are fabulous days out; learning and appreciating the vastness of His creation. Imagination, dreams and visions are developed in an atmosphere where there are no limitations to the vastness of exploration that can be undertaken.

The development of each child in Heaven is taken very seriously indeed. The gifts and callings bestowed upon a child before the foundation of the world are not hindered whatsoever by a limited time on Earth. For this is borne out in Romans 11:29 where it says,

> *"For God's gifts and His call are irrevocable. (He never withdraws them once they are given, and He does not change His mind about those to whom He gives His grace, or to whom He sends His call.)"*

All children will develop in the God-ordained purpose and plan that was prepared for them before the very foundation of Earth. God has created us all as unique beings in the largest and most complex array of architecture: the history of all humanity. We are living stones, and yet we are part of the body of Christ, fulfilling our destinies and interacting with each other. The mystery and the magnificence of His creation are surely beyond our human understanding as we dwell upon the truths of who we are in the Scriptures. We cannot underestimate the magnificence, the overwhelming generosity and grace with which He has bestowed upon us - everything that we might ever need.

In the light of all He has designed - How much more is He going to take care of the little ones…!

Chapter Ten

Encounter with Jesus

I found myself looking again into the heavenly realm from what could only be with spiritual eyes, seeing beyond and listening to the instructive whispers of Holy Spirit in my innermost being, as I clearly heard Him describing a heavenly dialogue between my mum and her sister.

To put some understanding into this, my auntie Doreen (my mum's sister) was born several years before my mum, but due to an illness, only survived until she was six weeks old. I want to give reassurance again to those who have lost children, for whatever reason and say that all infants, upon leaving this Earth realm, will without a question of doubt, pass on and continue living in Heaven to be reunited with families who have passed on before. They will await the glorious reunion of those yet to be promoted to Heaven; those who have accepted salvation.

The dialogue starts...

"Dearest Doreen, dearest sister," my mum begins saying, "this is the most beautiful place that I've ever experienced.

A Glimpse into Heaven

I feel so comfortable here: I feel so happy and content. I feel so complete. I feel like I have lived here forever. All that is around me is familiar; all that I am doing feels like it has been made especially for me. It is like every thread of the tapestry of my life on Earth has been woven into the most beautiful of beautiful surroundings; the most beautiful of beautiful love songs are continually playing in my ears and have been especially written for me... and the most beautiful of beautiful fragrances surround me wherever I go."

"Dearest Dee, you do make me laugh!" answers Doreen, "I love getting to know you. For I have grown up here, ever since I came here as a baby, but you have spent all this time in the Earth realm and gained so many valuable experiences and touched so many precious souls in your time there. I feel that although we have lived such different lives, we will be so close and benefit together from our different backgrounds. You, Dee, have only been here in your heavenly home for a few short Earth months, and you have only experienced the tiniest fraction of the infinite experiences and pleasures of Heaven." She continues, "Just wait until you meet Jesus! This will be the most glorious experience. It will be then that you understand considerably more than now the workings of Heaven. There is nothing that compares to His countenance, His wisdom and His love. After being in His presence for just a fraction of a second, you will be totally bowled over by everything about Him. Oh my, truly He is the centre of all life, the very essence of the Father's love, which radiates from every pore and expression of His being."

Doreen continues, "And Dee, I have been so excited to meet you, my dearest sister, I could hardly contain myself when I heard that you were coming and that your days on Earth were short. I was beside myself with excitement. I have, of course, been asking all your friends and family here, who knew you on Earth, what you like, so that I could do, "the big sister thing" and ensure that your new home would be filled with every type of dainty that you would enjoy. Do tell me little sis - can I call you "little sis"? is all of this to your pleasing? "

"Sweetest Doreen, you certainly have taken so much trouble in arranging, planning and preparing my beautiful home."

Doreen then continues by asking, "And how is your work with the children? How are you enjoying this? Do you feel fulfilled in this assignment?"

"Oh yes, Doreen," replies my mum, "I'm so very privileged to be given such a precious task; I just want to do my very best for these dear little ones, to see them grow and flourish in all that has been created for them."

The dialogue then ended and Holy Spirit began to expound upon aspects within the conversation that I had just heard.

After someone has been in Heaven for a period of time and has experienced sufficient rest and restoration, they will be given an assignment to attend to. The timing of these assignments is totally dependent upon the individual and the spiritual growth in and among their new surroundings.

Assignments are often in line with and a continuation of one's hobbies, desires, or work that was done on the Earth.

However, obviously, not everyone found a vocation on Earth in line with their desires. The assignments are not onerous but are fulfilling and a delightful part of life in Heaven. Everyone is so grateful and so overwhelmingly thankful for their salvation, surroundings and life, and therefore the whole emphasis is very much on how to bless others, give to others and grow in every aspect of life in the kingdom of Heaven.

I was delighted when the Spirit of God informed me that my mum would be assisting in taking charge of some children of kindergarten age. I felt so privileged that the Spirit of God was communicating this to me, and I was overjoyed as I knew how much my mother would excel in this task and would revel in the privilege of such an assignment.

As I received a glimpse of this assignment, I will do my best to describe the details that I saw...

It was a glorious summer's afternoon in Heaven. I saw my mum sitting under a huge tree in a garden or park-like area. Around her were about fifteen or so little three-year-olds.

All around, for as far as the eye could see, I saw blades of grass, shimmering and supporting what could only be described as crystals. These crystal-like balls were about five inches in diameter, opaque and the most exquisite colours. Some were amber, some sapphire, whilst others were multicoloured; they radiated the light that hit them turning the surface into a glowing rainbow effect of light, cascading in all directions. The children were having the most amazing time running through, capturing and releasing these crystals, as they took them in their tiny hands and let them float off into the atmosphere. There were squeals of excited laughter as they played with and through these light projecting gems.

I could only liken this to the past time on Earth of blowing bubbles from a soap solution, but this was vastly more fun and entertaining. After a while the gems all disappeared, and the children turned their attention to my mother.

The children sat on the grass together, randomly spread in front of my mum and seemingly listening intently to what was being taught. This was interrupted every so often by pockets of excited laughter and giggles that erupted and spread throughout the little gathering.

The children were all so well behaved, beautifully dressed and turned out, and seemingly of various different nationalities and cultures.

I feel so excited, overwhelmed and privileged to describe the next part of the scene that I was shown as it has been impressed into my spirit. As we are all governed by this earth realm, obviously there is no vocabulary and grammatical eloquence that exists that can fully express this heavenly scene in all its quality and brilliance. However, I believe that as you allow Holy Spirit to paint the picture also in your spirit, He will fill in the gaps. This is my favourite part of the book so far.

As the children's lesson continued, in the distance could be heard the noise of further merriment and excitement. I looked away to this noise for a moment, and when my gaze returned back to the lesson, I saw that it was beginning to come to an end. To my surprise, the children, in absolute, complete unison, had also turned their attention and were seemingly mesmerised by a figure coming towards them along the path that bordered the grass area. It was not clear who was interrupting the lesson and the little gathering on the grass. However, the children all looked longingly at the figure, waiting in silent obedience for a beckoning or a gesture. As the footsteps of the individual grew closer, there was a crispness of sound underfoot, even though the ground was not frosty; every footfall could be distinctly heard and seemed to reverberate for miles in both directions. Although it was a clear, beautiful, brilliant summer's day, the light that streamed all around this individual was overwhelmingly consuming. All along the path was an excited, chattering noise, coming from the plants, as each one seemingly turned its bloom or blossom to caress the extreme light that glowed far greater than anything of the noon-day sun. Every blade of grass, even though manicured to absolute perfection, seemed to straighten up, almost to attention, and joined the assembly of excited commotion. It was not long before the figure came into view and the children received their invitation to approach.

I looked into His eyes... His eyes were compassion and love personified, with an overriding sense of all-knowing and wisdom. His eyes were as blue as the Aegean Sea and seemed to go down to the depths of all infinity. There was no need for the spoken word or any motion or gesture, for He spoke a thousand words with His eyes in a single moment. His smile was strong and all-embracing and totally inclusive, giving full reassurance of the magnitude of His love. His hands expressed such warmth and strength which gave anyone in His presence the touch of reassurance and encouragement; likened only to that of a thousand hugs and kisses between lovers. His voice was beyond all understanding and pierced the Heavens with such clarity and distinct communication. His voice did not boom, but radiated with love and compassion, pulsating through eternity with every syllable that He uttered, resounding through the eons of time, never coming to an end.

He then beckoned the children, without any motion or gesture whatsoever, but instead with a look that simply said, "I love you" and "come to me."

A Glimpse into Heaven

All the children ran to Him, laughing and squealing with such excited joyfulness. His arms were held out now, beckoning them towards Himself. As they ran to Him, they piled into Him in a way that only children can. In just one moment of time, He responded to each child individually. One by one, He acknowledged each child by name. And as He spoke the name of each child, He spoke their name with such excitement and love, embracing each with a hug of total affection and tenderness. As I glimpsed further into this scene, I noticed that there were some children, whom He referred to as "my beautiful little darling" or "my handsome young man" with no less affection than those He had spoken to by their name. I questioned the Spirit as to why some children were not beckoned with their name. The answer came that some parents had never named their child before they passed on into Heaven but they were however no less loved and doted over by Him. He loves the children - He really loves the children.

> His voice did not boom, but radiated with love and compassion, pulsating through eternity with every syllable that He uttered resounding through the eons of time, never coming to an end.

Without any words, He looked at my mum and the words that emanated from His eyes were: "Thank you for looking after my little ones. Thank you. You are doing a good work and I'm grateful".

All Hail the Lamb!!

Chapter Eleven

A Glimpse of the Workings of Praise

I was in a weekly praise evening where the majority of my local church was assembled. There was a group of the worship team leading the praise when I received what I can only describe as a glimpse of the "workings of praise". I believe every sincere Christian wants to have further insight into how praise and worship upon this Earth reaches the heavenlies, its purpose and its course to the throne of God.

There is a connection between praise upon the earth, above the Earth and in the heavens and an amalgamation of praise working in unison in all these realms. Just as it says in Psalm 69:34,

> *"Let the heaven and earth, praise him, the seas and everything that moveth therein".*

Here, it clearly states praise is both in Heaven and on Earth and not just one or the other!

Psalm 148 continues to describe how praise originates from every realm and everything,

> *"Praise the Lord from the heavens, praise Him in the heights! Praise Him all His angels, praise Him, all His hosts! Praise Him, sun and moon, praise Him, all you stars of light! All praise Him, you highest heavens, and you waters above the heavens!... Praise the Lord from the earth... Let them praise and exalt the name of the Lord for His name alone is exalted and supreme! His glory and majesty are above earth and heaven!"*

There is nothing under the sound of His voice that should not praise Him.

That evening, I sat quietly mesmerised by the beauty of the worship in a place where I was completely focused on Him and the things above. I felt such gratitude to the Spirit of God for all the sweetest of revelations I had been so privileged to have shared thus far and as I did, I asked Holy Spirit whether there were further scenes that He wanted to reveal to me. As I continued to sit there, I felt impressed to start scribbling in my notebook, as I had done on so many occasions previously. As I did, I glimpsed into the heavens and allowed my spirit to soar. I relaxed and drank in the tranquillity of the moment. As I began to see into this realm, I heard the following dialogue:

"Hi, it's me, Doreen, how are you, Dee? Are you in?"

"Yes, yes," came the reply, as she ran to the door and embraced her sister.

"These are for you, Dee," she continued as she held out a huge bunch of living roses. The blooms were massive, and each petal was perfectly sculpted with the appearance of the most thick, luxurious velvety substance, extremely soft to the touch. In a moment, the fragrances of these blooms had pervaded and filled the entire hallway with their magnificent scent.

"Come, come, let's go onto the veranda - can I make you a drink?" she continued. The two sat there exchanging thoughts, laughing and enjoying the tranquillity and peaceful ambience of the cool of the day.

After a few moments, Doreen commented, "So you met our most wonderful Saviour today, Dee. Tell me about your encounter – isn't He just beyond words?"

My mum turned her face intently towards Doreen and her face began to glow with excitement as she recalled that special moment. "Yes, yes," replied my mum. "I saw His scarred hands… I saw His scarred feet. Oh Doreen, I was mesmerised…" Her eyes twinkled with elation and delight and a greater sense of peace started to radiate from her entire body, as she took her hands up and grasped them tightly to her chest as she continued. "I was totally overwhelmed by His presence… in fact Doreen, I am still processing all that took place, as it was far beyond any experience I have ever known." She seemed profoundly affected with this encounter and she gave a deep reflective sign.

The two ladies continued to sit in quiet contemplation of the events of the day.

Then Doreen said, "Could you ever have imagined what

Heaven was like Dee, whilst you were living on Earth?"

"No, no, not at all, dearest Doreen," came the reply.

Doreen continued, "What has been the one aspect of Heaven that has surprised you the most or made the greatest impression on you?"

Without hesitation, my mum answered, "I never realised that praise is the very heartbeat of Heaven. Praise can erupt at any moment in any situation in Heaven and frequently does, as I see individuals and groups of people overwhelmed by the God of love, who only knows to bless us all abundantly as an expression of His love. Praise has got to be the most electrifying, all-consuming force that I never realised was so incredibly overpowering and an all-inclusive mechanism in Heaven." This was such an awesome account of the astounding workings of praise, that both ladies paused in their conversation, simply savouring the words and phrases that had just been uttered.

I then received from Holy Spirit such a beautiful illustration of the workings of praise; something I find both comforting as well as exponentially exhilarating.

Words are full of creative substance; but praise is full of heavenly substance. Praise was ordained in the very heart of God.

The ability to praise is in the heart of every created human being. Praise and adoration are only released out of a pure heart. A heart that is stubborn, unyielding and unforgiving is not ready to adore, magnify or glorify Him. Conversely, a pure heart; a heart that is overflowing with gratitude and thankfulness, is a heart from which true praise is produced and is created, fashioned and released upon its journey to the heavenly city of God. This is a heart that is soft and yielding to Holy Spirit. This is where the full expression of one's gratitude and exuberance before God is released in the pure essence of an aroma of praise - the ingredient to change mere words into powerful instruments of worship.

This is the same type of heart Mary Magdalene had, when she poured the oil from the alabaster jar and washed Jesus's feet with her hair. With such tenderness and loving adoration, she gave unselfishly to Him. We do not need to be able to sing in tune or understand the intricacies of music: we just need to come before Him with a pure heart and, figuratively speaking, pour forth "all" in worship at His feet.

As the worship continued in the church evening of praise, I saw the group of Christians, praising God in unison, giving Him adoration and exalting Him in song. Their worship, their words, their voices and their harmonies merged together, melting the very heart of the listener and bringing all who heard the sound into a place of surrender. As the male and female voices sang to differing melodies and harmonised in different verses, it was as if the weapons of praise seemed to exponentially increase against the forces of darkness, whose array was scattered in absolute confusion as the distinct praises radiated out into the skies.

> Words are full of creative substance.
>
> But praise is full of heavenly substance.

A Glimpse into Heaven

There is no pure praise without the manifestation of a magnificent light show! How do I start to explain such an orchestral, galactic, terrestrial extravaganza? As I looked further, I saw a new realm; I saw a new dimension. The anointed worship seemed to go "up a notch", as the participants had reached a place of total surrender as they were abandoned to the beauty of the moment. It was as if we had climbed a set of steps, turned and saw the panoramic and spectacular view from a new vantage point. But now the real show began!

I saw a spectacle of lights. Yellowy orange swirls of light emanated from within the praise that had just been released, as if the patterned lights were engulfed within the praise they were travelling in. Then, as the other harmonious voices entered into the ensemble, the source of light became multicoloured and danced in a multi-patterned display. I suppose this is not surprising when we consider that sound travels in waves, and colour uses the electromagnetic spectrum in a range of frequencies of different lengths.

Next, I turned my attention to the skies, above the little gathering of worshippers. The skies were filled with angelic beings, far too many to count. Innumerable angels, on assignment, were participating, enjoying and reveling in these worship activities. I could see streams of light travelling from one corner of the sky to another, as the angels "dive-bombed" the expanse of sky in an aerobatic display of supernatural ability. They were weaving in and out in a demonstration of graceful agility, somewhat likened to that of the "Red Arrows" flying display team. It seemed that this was a completely natural activity with no time restraints and could have continued on forever without ceasing.

Beyond our earthly skies, I peeked into Heaven, in my mind's eye. The worshippers on Earth pushed deeper into His presence and further into sheer adoration with undivided attention upon Him, with no earthly agenda whatsoever.

In this place, I saw some inhabitants of Heaven, erupting in worship as they leant over the balustrades of Heaven to peak at the spectacle below. Additionally, a light spectacle in the skies above the heavens, of such majestic proportions; unlimited and radiating colours outside of our spectrum was moving and traversing as far as the eye could see. It could only be described as a likeness, in the northern hemisphere, to that of the Aurora Borealis, but of far superior grandeur and magnificence.

There is a place in worship on Earth, where we know that all of the hosts of Heaven, together with the angelic assembly, join in as one, as the fragrance of corporate worship is poured forth before the very throne of God. What a sweet-smelling aroma infuses into the heavenly city!

What a privilege that praise and worship, originating from the heart of man, can escalate to the throne of God, and upon its journey can encapsulate and mobilise the angelic hosts in the skies and the very inhabitants, who we know in Heaven.

What an absolute privilege we have at our disposal! What amazing reassurance, as we have a glimpse of Heaven, and seek, in our mind's eye, loved ones, entering into His presence with a jubilant expression of praise and adoration. We are as one together, all creation, in complete unity, with corporate praise bringing forth adoration unceasingly before Him.

I saw Doreen, turn back to look at her sister. She noticed a small tear in her eye.

Dee, noticing her gaze, said, "My loved ones on Earth, although I miss them, when they praise our God, they are entering into the smallest and yet the largest part of my world in Heaven, and when they do, I just love it!" She continued, "One of my favourite places to visit is the arrival portal; the place that is referred to as the balustrades of Heaven, where we can take a peek at the Earth beneath. I remember the day that I first met you, Doreen when you greeted me there as my new sister. I love to see praise reverberating through the eons of the ages, through the cosmic radiance of lightheaded straight to the throne of God, to worship Him who is truly the Alpha and the Omega and the very essence of all life."

Let everything that has breath, praise the Lord! What a magnificent, loving Father we have! What an awesome Saviour we have! What a super future we have!

Thank you for taking the time out of your busy schedule to read this book, my earnest, heartfelt prayer is that this book has brought you closer to the Father into a greater intimacy with the Lord Jesus Christ and walking and hearing the Holy Spirit in a greater capacity than ever before. That there has been healing and restoration by the great physician himself and a knowledge that loved ones in Heaven are cheering you on, as you fulfil the number of your days on earth, as they wait patiently for the sweetest of homecomings.

A Glimpse of the Workings of Praise

A Glimpse into Heaven

Salvation Prayer

As I come to the end of this book, I realise that some readers will be asking questions such as: "How can I have such a relationship with God to hear such amazing things" or "How do I know that I will one day go to Heaven – is this possible for me?"

Please let me explain that the life that we live is more than just flesh and more than just a bodily experience. The life that we live can be impacted on a daily basis by the Lord Jesus Christ in a most life giving and miraculous way.

The entrance into living a supernatural life is firstly a commitment to ask the Lord Jesus Christ into our life. To recognise that it is only through His dying on the cross for our sins that we can come into a relationship with our Heavenly Father.

Choosing to receive the Lord Jesus Christ is the most important decision you will ever make on this Earth.

God's word promises us in Romans 10:9-10 and 13,

> *"that if you confess with your mouth the Lord Jesus and believe in your heart that God has raised Him from the dead, you will be saved. For with the heart man believes unto righteousness, and with the mouth confession is made unto salvation."*
>
> *"For whoever calls on the name of the Lord shall be saved."*

God has already done everything to provide salvation for us because of His amazing love and grace towards us. But now we have a part of play which is to believe and receive.

Please read this simple prayer out loud; speaking it with all your heart:

> *"*Jesus, I believe that you died on a cross for me and I believe in my heart that God raised You from the dead. I confess that You are my Lord and Saviour. By faith in Your Word, I receive salvation now. Thank you for saving me and giving me new life. Amen*"*

The very instant you commit your life to Jesus Christ, He responds to you and the truth of His Word immediately comes to pass in your innermost being; your spirit. Now you are a born-again believer and a new creation – He has made you, a brand-new you! And you have the assurance that when you leave this Earth, you will continue to live on throughout eternity in Heaven – yes, the Heaven that you have been reading about.

Praise God!

About the Author

Jenny, and her husband Darren, are passionate about sharing the good news of the Gospel, with signs and wonders following the teaching of the Word of God.

They have a heart for teaching and evangelism – seeing people saved, baptized in the Holy Spirit, healed and set free from bondage.

Special thanks to Madeleine W Pires
Madeleine is a wonderful friend of ours. We first met in a lovely church in Manchester.

With her understanding of the English language, as a professional teacher, Madeleine has helped me to communicate the message of this book into written form.

It has been invaluable to discuss, sometimes at length, the message received from Holy Spirit, and to correctly portray it, grammatically, for the reader.

I am very grateful indeed for her beautiful illustrations which capture a part of my mind's eye view of Heaven.

Printed in Great Britain
by Amazon